I Like Apples!

WAYLAND

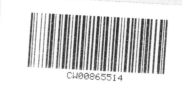

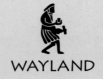

First published in 2011
by Wayland

Text copyright © Claire Llewellyn
Photograph copyright © Wayland
with the exception of: cover background © Istock, graphic p10 © Istock
and graphic p16 © Istock

Wayland
338 Euston Road
London NW1 3BH

Wayland Australia
Level 17/207 Kent Street
Sydney, NSW 2000

Series Editor: Louise John
Editor: Katie Powell
Design: D.R.ink
Photographer: Andy Crawford
Consultant: Shirley Bickler

A CIP catalogue record for this book is available from the British Library.

ISBN 9780750263795

Printed in China

Wayland is a division of Hachette Children's Books,
an Hachette UK Company.
www.hachette.co.uk

Contents

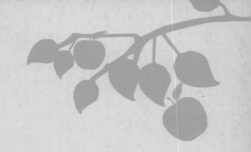

I need food!

I need food and water.

They keep my body
working well.

My food

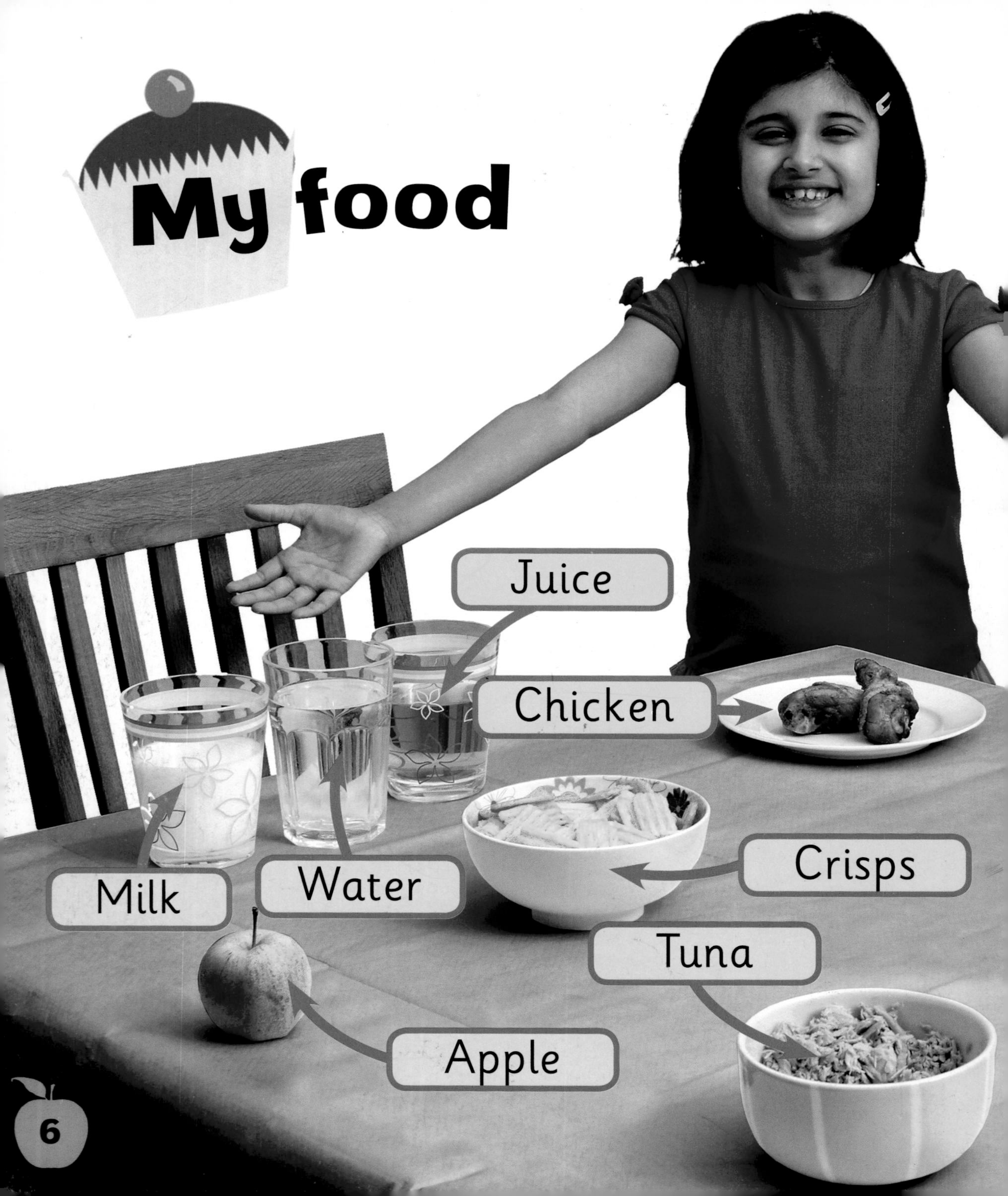
Juice
Chicken
Milk
Water
Crisps
Tuna
Apple

Here are some of the things
I like to eat and drink.

They taste good.

I like apples

Mum says:

Fruit helps to keep you well.

I eat lots of fruit.
I like apples the best.

I like peas

Mum always puts vegetables on my plate at dinner.

Today I am having peas.
I like peas the best.

Mum says:

Vegetables are good for you.

I love pasta

Some foods are good
at filling me up.

Mum says:

Food like pasta gives you energy.

I like them all
but I **love** pasta.

I love cheese

Every day I have meat
or fish or cheese or eggs.

Mum says:

All these foods help you to grow.

I **love** to eat cheese.

The best meals

I like these meals the best...

but I only have them
now and then.

It's a treat

I like to eat sweets, cakes and ice cream.

Mum says:

Sweet foods are bad for your teeth.

I sometimes have them as a treat.

Drink up!

I need to drink every day.

Orange squash

Water

Apple juice

Milk

I like water the best.

Mum says:
Water and milk are good for you, so drink them every day.

My favourite foods

Look at all this food and drink.

Which things do you like to eat?

Which things do you like to drink?

Which things do you not like?

Milk, water and apple juice

Apple

Chicken and rice

Jacket potato and salad

Fish and chips

Spaghetti bolognaise

Cake

Ice cream

START READING is a series of highly enjoyable books for beginner readers. **The books have been carefully graded to match the Book Bands widely used in schools.** This enables readers to be sure they choose books that match their own reading ability.

Look out for the Band colour on the book in our Start Reading logo.

The Bands are:

- Pink Band 1A & 1B
- Red Band 2
- Yellow Band 3
- Blue Band 4
- Green Band 5
- Orange Band 6
- Turquoise Band 7
- Purple Band 8
- Gold Band 9

START READING books can be read independently or shared with an adult. They promote the enjoyment of reading through satisfying stories and non-fiction narratives, which are supported by fun illustrations and photographs.

Claire Llewellyn has written many books for children. Some of them are about real things like animals and the Moon, others are storybooks. Claire has two children, but they are getting too big for her books now. She hopes you will enjoy reading them instead!